The True Story of

THE BATTLE OF THE ALAMO

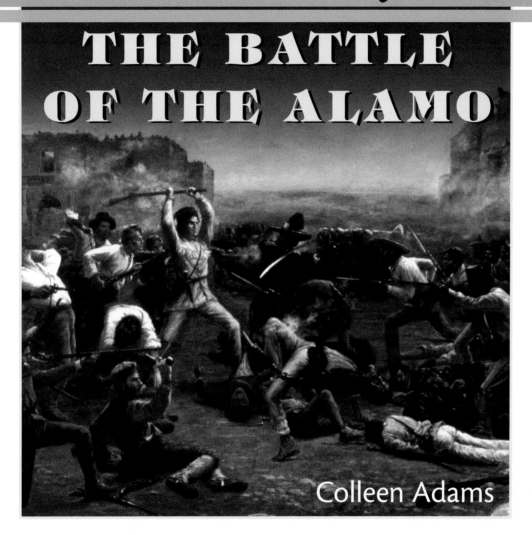

Colleen Adams

PowerKiDS
press.

New York

Published in 2009 by The Rosen Publishing Group, Inc.
29 East 21st Street, New York, NY 10010

First Edition

Editor: Nicole Pristash
Book Design: Kate Laczynski
Photo Researcher: Nicole Pristash

Photo Credits: Cover, pp. 1, 19 © Getty Images, Inc.; pp. 5, 7 Shutterstock.com; pp. 9, 11, 13 © Bettmann/Corbis; pp. 15, 21 © Superstock.com; p. 17 © North Wind/North Wind Picture Archives.

Library of Congress Cataloging-in-Publication Data

Adams, Colleen.
  The true story of the Battle of the Alamo / Colleen Adams.
    p. cm. — (What really happened?)
  Includes bibliographical references and index.
  ISBN 978-1-4042-4477-1 (library binding)
  1. Alamo (San Antonio, Tex.)—Siege, 1836—Juvenile literature. I. Title.
  F390.A206 2009
  976.4'03—dc22

                                        2008000997

Manufactured in the United States of America

CONTENTS

What Is the Alamo? 4

Trouble in Texas 6

Santa Anna Takes Charge 8

The Army of the People 10

Alone in Battle? 12

Outnumbered 14

The Last Fight 16

Independence 18

Davy Crockett's Death..20

What Really Happened? 22

Glossary 23

Index 24

Web Sites...24

WHAT IS THE ALAMO?

Have you ever heard of the Alamo? The Alamo is a place in San Antonio, Texas, where a famous battle took place in 1836. During the Texas **Revolution**, the people of Texas fought against the Mexican Army. They fought to win their **independence** from Mexico. During the battle, Texas became free and became its own state.

There are many questions surrounding the battle of the Alamo and one of the men who fought there. Let's take a look at some of these stories and find out what really happened!

You can visit the Alamo and walk through the buildings where the battle took place. More than two million people visit the Alamo every year.

TROUBLE IN TEXAS

The story begins in the 1820s. At this time, Texas was a Mexican state, named Tejas (TAY-has). The Mexicans who lived there were called Tejanos (teh-HA-nos). At this time, many Americans were moving into Tejas. These Americans were called Texians because they called the land Texas.

The government would not allow the people of Texas to grow cotton. People could make a lot of money growing cotton. Many thought this law was unfair.

The Mexican government had a lot of rules for the Tejanos and the new Texians coming from America.

One rule said that all people in Mexico had to be **Catholic**. Texians could not practice their own **religion**, which angered them very much.

In 1821, Mexico gained its independence from Spain. This map shows what Mexico looked like during that time.

SANTA ANNA TAKES CHARGE

In 1830, the Mexican government made a law banning more Americans from coming into Texas. The government had also banned **slavery**. Many of the Texians and Tejanos were slave owners, and they did not want to follow this law.

Three years later, in 1833, a Mexican general, named Antonio López de Santa Anna, became president of Mexico. Santa Anna took over and made even more laws that people thought were unfair. Some people believe that the Tejanos agreed with their government. However, the Tejanos were not happy with these laws, either. The people of Texas wanted to rule themselves, and they were ready to take on the government.

Santa Anna was afraid the United States was going to try to take over Texas. To take control, Santa Anna made laws that many people did not agree with.

9

THE ARMY OF THE PEOPLE

Santa Anna had a plan to control the people of Texas. He believed if he took all the **weapons** away from the Texians, they could not start a revolution.

On October 2, 1835, 100 men from the Mexican Army came to the town of Gonzales, Texas. The army tried to take away a **cannon** the town owned. Instead, the Texians fired the cannon, which sent the Mexican Army away. This was known as the battle of Gonzales. It was the start of the Texas Revolution. Soon, **volunteers** in Texas formed their own army called the Army of the People.

Many members of the Army of the People were not fighters but family men. Here some of the men are seen with one of the army's leaders, William Travis (right).

ALONE IN BATTLE?

In November 1835, the Army of the People and the Mexican Army gathered at the Alamo. A fight broke out. Texas won, but Santa Anna did not give up. Two months later, Santa Anna came back with more than 5,000 men. William Travis, leader of the troops at the Alamo, sent messages to other leaders, asking for more people to come and **defend** the Alamo.

One story says that Travis drew a line in the sand and asked those who wanted to fight to cross it. All but one person did. It is not known if this really happened.

Many believe that no one tried to help, and the defenders had to fight alone. However, it has been proven that help was on the way. One colonel in the Texas army tried to lead 320 men to help Travis. However, he was unsuccessful.

This picture shows the Mexican Army arriving at the Alamo with their guns and cannons. The Mexican Army was better prepared than the Texas army.

13

OUTNUMBERED

The members of the Mexican Army greatly outnumbered the defenders in the Texas army. Both armies fired shots at each other day after day. The Mexican Army hoped the defenders would give up and leave the Alamo. The Texas army refused, though.

Davy Crockett was one of the men who fought at the Alamo. During this time, Crockett was known all over Texas. He was famous for his outdoor and shooting skills.

Then, on March 1, after eight long days of waiting, 32 Texians made it to the Alamo to help the defenders. This brought the number of defenders at the Alamo to more than 200. This new group was known as the **Immortal** 32. They were the only men who arrived in time to help defend the Alamo.

The Alamo defenders (right) were strong in their beliefs. They believed that if they could fight off the Mexican Army (left), they could be free of Mexico's rule.

THE LAST FIGHT

After 13 days of firing shots and waiting, Santa Anna ordered his men to **attack** the Alamo on March 6, 1836. The Mexican Army attacked from four different directions. The defenders fought back. However, the large Mexican Army soon tore down the walls of the Alamo and fired inside. The Army of the People fought hard, but they did not win.

One of the stories that many people believe is that all the Texians and Tejanos at the Alamo died that day. This is not true. About 15 to 20 people lived through the terrible battle. They were women, children, and one slave.

Here the Mexican Army is seen using ladders to climb through the windows of the Alamo. This helped the army get inside to overpower the defenders.

17

INDEPENDENCE

While the battle was going on, Texas leaders met to work toward **separating** Texas from Mexico. They wanted to break away by voting and withdrawing Texas from Mexico's government. On March 2, 1836, while the battle went on, Texas became the **Republic** of Texas.

Some people believe that the defenders of the Alamo died for nothing because Texas became independent before the last attack happened. It is likely that the defenders did not know Texas had become independent. However, they had sent their leaders to meet before the battle began, so they knew independence was coming.

Even though Texas became free during the battle, the defenders' brave fighting showed the Mexican government that they would not give up.

19

DAVY CROCKETT'S DEATH

The biggest mystery about the Alamo is how Davy Crockett died. It is believed that he died while fighting inside the Alamo. Because of this, Crockett became a symbol, or sign, of the Alamo's brave defenders. However, in 1955, a journal was found that suggested that the Mexican Army took Crockett and six other men. The journal states that members of the Mexican Army killed Crockett and the other men at a different spot.

How Davy Crockett died is one of the biggest questions that have come about since the battle. We may never know the truth about this hero's last moments.

Davy Crockett became famous for his part in helping defend the Alamo. A song about his life was written in the 1950s. The song is called "The Ballad of Davy Crockett."

WHAT REALLY HAPPENED?

There are many different stories about the battle of the Alamo. Some stories have questions that can be answered. Other stories leave us wondering what really happened. Did the Tejanos and Texians disagree with one another? Were the defenders left alone to die for nothing? Did Davy Crockett die fighting like a hero?

Even if we never know the whole truth, the Alamo will always be remembered. The battle shows how strong a small army of men can be. They were not afraid to fight to be free. Because of this, they became an important part of history.

GLOSSARY

attack (uh-TAK) To start a fight with.

cannon (KA-nun) A large, heavy gun.

Catholic (KATH-lik) Someone who belongs to the Roman Catholic faith.

defend (dih-FEND) To guard.

immortal (ih-MOR-tul) Always living.

independence (in-dih-PEN-dents) The state of being free from the control of other people.

religion (rih-LIH-jen) A belief in and a way of honoring a god or gods.

republic (rih-PUH-blik) A form of government in which people choose representatives to run the government.

revolution (reh-vuh-LOO-shun) A change in government.

separating (SEH-puh-rayt-ing) Breaking apart from something.

slavery (SLAY-vuh-ree) When one person owns another.

volunteers (vah-lun-TEERZ) People who give their time without pay.

weapons (WEH-punz) Object or tools used to hurt or kill.

INDEX

A
Americans, 6, 8

I
independence, 4, 18

L
leader(s), 12, 18

M
Mexican Army, 4, 10, 12, 14, 16, 20
Mexico, 4, 6, 8, 18

R
Republic of Texas, 18

S
San Antonio, Texas, 4
Santa Anna, Antonio López de, 8, 10, 12, 16
slavery, 8
state, 4, 6

T
Tejanos, 6, 8, 16, 22

Tejas, 6
Texas, 4, 6, 8, 10, 12, 14, 18
Texas Revolution, 4, 10
Texians, 6, 8, 10, 14, 16, 22
Travis, William, 12

V
volunteers, 10

W
weapons, 10

WEB SITES

Due to the changing nature of Internet links, PowerKids Press has developed an online list of Web sites related to the subject of this book. This site is updated regularly. Please use this link to access the list:
www.powerkidslinks.com/wrh/alamo/